From Flitch to Ash
A Musing on Trees and Carving

Alice Street Editions
Judith P. Stelboum
Editor-in-Chief

From Flitch to Ash: A Musing on Trees and Carving, by Diane Derrick

Treat, by Angie Vicars

Yin Fire, by Alexandra Grilikhes

His Hands, His Tools, His Sex, His Dress: Lesbian Writers on Their Fathers, edited by Catherine Reid and Holly K. Iglesias

Weeding at Dawn: A Lesbian Country Life, by Hawk Madrone

Façades, by Alex Marcoux

Inside Out, by Juliet Carrera

Past Perfect, by Judith P. Stelboum

Forthcoming

Your Loving Arms, by Gwendolyn Bikis

Egret, by Helen Collins

Back to Salem, by Alex Marcoux

Extraordinary Couples, Ordinary Lives, by Lynn Haley-Banez and Joanne Garrett

Advance praise for Diane Derrick's

From Flitch to Ash: A Musing on Trees and Carving

"*From Flitch to Ash* contains images which were originally sculptures but have been digitized to look like nineteenth-century book illustrations. The text reveals the artist's journey into wood carving and the devastating loss of her work to fire. After a period of recovery, she began to work in clay. Central to the book are Derrick's commentaries on the spirituality of wood and wilderness and the nature of forests."

–Tee A. Corrine, *FABB: The Feminist Art Books Bulletin*

"A beautifully wrought tale of personal transformation in the face of profound loss, of a spiritual journey begun by necessity and continuing in the heady lightness of freedom from the past. Sometimes the goddess must know that it takes a disaster to spur us to the changes we most resist. Derrick's sparse and elegant prose . . . buoys the reader on waves of language crafted as dearly as her lost wooden sculptures of undraped women."

–Hawk Madrone, author of *Weeding at Dawn*

"Important. . . . In telling the story of a fire that tragically turned her entire body of work into smoke, Derrick shapes her memories and forms her emotionally based theories with great tenderness, much like her new-found clay, leaving soft handprints on her readers' hearts. The illustrations [of her woodcarvings] pay tribute to female boldness, sensuality, and playfulness. . . . When a person experiences great loss, and allows grief to follow its course, it is the grief that can tell an artist where to make the next right mark. [This book] is just that mark."

–Lorraine Inzalaco, MFA, studio artist; author of "Visible for a Change," *HLFQ 1*(1)

Foreword

Alice Street Editions provides a voice for established as well as up-coming lesbian writers, reflecting the diversity of lesbian interests, ethnicities, ages and class. This cutting edge series of novels, memoirs, and non-fiction writing welcomes the opportunity to present controversial views, explore multicultural ideas, encourage debate, and inspire creativity from a variety of lesbian perspectives. Through enlightening, illuminating and provocative writing, Alice Street Editions can make a significant contribution to the visibility and accessibility of lesbian writing, and bring lesbian-focused writing to a wider audience. Recognizing our own desires and ideas in print is life sustaining, acknowledging the reality of who we are, our place in the world, individually and collectively.

Judith P. Stelboum
Editor-in-Chief
Alice Street Editions

Published by

Alice Street Editions, Harrington Park Press®, an imprint of The Haworth Press, Inc.,
10 Alice Street, Binghamton, NY 13904-1580 USA. (www.HaworthPress.com)

Cover design by Thomas J. Mayshock Jr.

Cover art by Diane Derrick. *Woman on a Turtle*, detail.

Library of Congress Cataloging-in-Publication Data

Derrick, Diane, 1934-
    From flitch to ash: a musing on trees and carving / Diane Derrick.
      p. cm.
    ISBN 1-56023-216-1 (alk. paper)–ISBN 1-56023-217-X (pbk : alk. paper)
      1. Derrick, Diane, 1934- 2. Sculptors–United States–Biography.
3. Wood sculpture, American. I. Title.

NB237.D487 A2 2001
730'.92–dc21
[B]   2001022486

From Flitch to Ash

A Musing on Trees and Carving

DIANE DERRICK

*To
Olivia*

Acknowledgments

Excerpts from the text and some of the plates were previously published in HLFQ–Harrington Lesbian Fiction Quarterly *and* Amazon Quarterly.

My thanks to Mina Meyer and Sharon Raphael for their encouraging support.

Contents

Prologue

For over twenty years I sculpted in wood and when a fire destroyed the work, my career as a carver came to an abrupt end. Even though friends and family assured me I'd soon resume carving, I knew I wouldn't for, besides the physical loss of the pieces, the fire also effectively stifled my creative impulse. I felt myself psychically stripped, sliding about on a glassy surface with no grips to grab, no toe holds to catch, but falling, sliding, blaming myself for making the ill-fated choices that led to the fire, slithering over the same slippery questions, repeating the same opaque answers.

With time, my mental squirming slowed, reality set in, and life such as it was went on. Eventually I did return to sculpture, but not to wood. It was the warmth and softness of clay that pulled me in a new direction. The old work was gone; there were no answers; that chapter was finished. From the start, clay seemed to transmit a joy to my fingers that gradually infused my being. As I modeled it up and squashed it down I felt relaxed and tranquil, feelings that surprised me. It was then I realized that on some deep level I had always felt an unease with wood. Perhaps it was the combination of hard physical work and razor sharp tools that kept my thoughts so focused, and I had accepted the underlying disquiet as a given of the complex process, the requisite tension inherent in creativity. Working with clay, however, soon dispelled that romantic notion of tension which, in fact, often acts more as hindrance than catalyst for ingenuity. There was something else, a missing link. My thoughts poised on the enigmatic medium of wood.

Through a fortuitous error in packing, I discovered a box of slides that had escaped the fire. It took a long time to even look at them again, but one day I spread them out. They looked strangely unfamiliar. I tried to recall my feelings as I carved, tried to remember what I had been thinking, what I had had in mind. But the process of carving is strenuous, and whatever accompanying emotions and ideas I had experienced didn't survive in my memory. The slides weren't talking. My mind returned again to the material itself, that inflammable medium that had seemed so formidable and impervious to my blows, and that had gone up in an all-consuming blaze leaving no trace of itself. One thing was clear: there was much about wood and trees I didn't understand. I knew little more about a block of wood than its physical properties of grain, color and density. It seemed amazing that it could have been my medium for so many years and yet I remained ignorant of its other qualities, especially of that ever-present faint discomfort whenever I worked. Those unhappy thoughts set my musings for this essay, and prompted me to face what I had steadfastly avoided in the past: an acknowledgment of the elemental force and mystical nature of wood.

The slides, I decided, would require altering to symbolize the change from objects existing in reality to residing in memory. As they were, they seemed to me a rogue's gallery of snapshots of dead relatives. Before the fire, the slides served as accessory to the work–inventory and record, and on occasion to submit for possible showings. Now, with no more inventory there would be no further shows, and the slides somehow lacked relevance. The solution came from looking at old engravings, black and white renderings with reference to a past but that also possessed a non-referential integrity of their own. The first step was to have the slides digitized, and from there I experimented with various effects until arriving at the line drawings as they appear here. My intent for this book has been to rescue the spirit of the work in terms of both text and illustration.

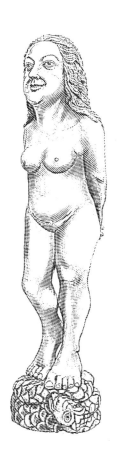

EVE

The Myth

When walking along a stretch of beach, one of life's subtle pleasures is to pick up a small piece of driftwood and slowly turn it in the palm of our hand, feel its smoothness, finger its whorls, learn its substance. Seduced by its sensual harmony, we embody the rhythm. We think better.

Wood touches a primordial nerve in the human psyche. Trees were here first, and the oldest not only predate our recorded history but also carry secrets of the earth we have yet to fathom. Deep in the forest, we sense a primitive and prehistoric presence

unruffled by the passage of time, a paradoxical aura
and one not confined to pristine nature, for artifacts
crafted of wood carry the mystique far beyond the
forest to span the centuries. Egyptian carvings emanate
a warmth and vitality of a culture long extinct yet
very much alive. Wood, the medium of transcendence,
doesn't die in our human sense but continues to ex-
pand and contract with the seasons and in millions
of years, under favorable conditions, will metamor-
phose into stone. And the little beach scrap of unknown origin and indeterminate age, tossed about
in the sea for who knows how long, provides a
grounding for our thoughts and binds us to the
eternal continuum.

BABY J

LADY ON A TURTLE

The Germ

No one knows who first picked up a stick and a flint and began to chip a little image, but it was most likely someone engaged in no more than whiling away a bit of time and whose fingers idly played with the objects at hand. Seeing the image emerge from her unpremeditated handiwork must have startled that first carver to the point of dropping both stone and stick and running through the forest as though possessed. That is how it is, the carver's moment of revelation: a baffling mix of power and awe and amazement at one's fingers acting independently of one's mind or, perhaps, in conjunction with the wood exerting a mind of its own. It's easy to slip into supernatural revery.

My first carving came in such a fashion. With new tools, I concentrated on practice, on creating nothing more than clean cuts and rhythmic chips when suddenly, unannounced and unforeseen, there she was, an awkward, homely little figure nestled in her wooden cocoon, a marvelous, wonderful, little miracle. My heart raced, my fingers shook and, forgetting practice and patience, I set to chopping her free and like Pygmalion, I expected her momentarily to gulp in a grateful breath of life.

Of course, she didn't, or if she did I was too busy to notice as that initial thrill had ignited a spark that spurred me to set free all little creatures entrapped in wooden cocoons. The spirits, I intuited, were with me.

*WISE & FOOLISH
VIRGINS*

The Spirits

The notion of spirits residing in wood and bursting to get out is as old as the forests. Many tribal carvers won't risk cutting down a tree without first receiving its permission, and it is not uncommon for present day indigenous effigy makers to find themselves banished from their communities to live and work isolated at a distant place, for who knows if the forces released from the wood will be good or evil, the image totem or taboo? It's not hard to believe. Meeting a fetish figure for the first time, even though it is encased behind glass, brings one face to face with a potent mix of maleficent vibes, and those who are wise don't take fetishes lightly. Years before I began to carve, in Oslo's Ethnological Museum I naively walked into an entire gallery of fetish figures: hundreds of wildly glaring agonized statues with exaggerated genitals, lumps and tumors, seared and singed, riddled with nails, stuck with glass shards and bits of mirror to reflect and direct their pain. Those fetishes transported from their origins, disoriented and lost, charged the atmosphere with a battering implosive energy. It was a frightening place, claustrophobic, airless and heavy, hard to breathe in, like fighting an undertow to move from case to case. Perhaps it is no coincidence that Munch's portrayals of isolation and inner terror hang in neighboring galleries, or that Vigeland's monoliths of tormented mankind writhe in nearby Frogner Park, or that the Norse woods and fjords abound with mercurial trolls.

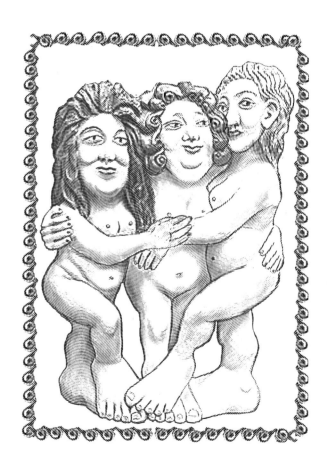

*HELEN, VIOLET
& EDNA*

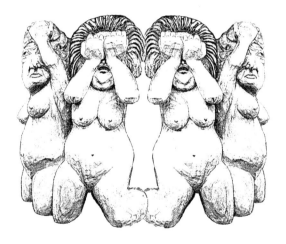

The Spell

Of course, not all effigies exude the malevolence of fetish figures. Most statues, however, and especially wooden ones, do arouse a curiosity. We search a sculpted face to read its promising silence. Is it just a copy or does the expression portend more? Can we learn from its frozen instant that which eludes us in our continuous rush? Some believe a portrait opens a window onto the soul, reveals a truth. With a statue we have time to stare and study and even touch, for the urge is often irresistible; instinctively our fingers reach out to connect. A communication passes between hand and object, a language of the senses that our intellect doesn't grasp. Guards patrol museum galleries ever alert to catch the over zealous, while much park and cemetery sculpture gleams worn and shiny from well-rubbed, hand-burnished ardor.

The potential impact of combining image with the mystical forces ingrained in the wood is formidable.

ST. MARK

MISS NUM

The Veil

The founding religious patriarchs knew well the potencies inherent in both nature and image. After all, art and religion share the same magical root, and, as well, address the same mystical concerns, albeit from radically different perspectives. Commonality of origin, of course, does not always make for compatibility. To the contrary, certain early mystagogues instinctively deemed art subversive and decreed an irrevocable prohibition of graven images, most likely fearing retribution from equivocal deities who might not take kindly to their earthly depiction, but also to ensure their following not be tempted by idolatry over orthodoxy. Other proselytizers took the opposite tact by deliberately blurring the line between idolatry and piety and embraced the magnetism of art precisely to enthrall their nascent flocks as well as to appease, flatter and glorify the gods–along with sundry saints and helpful patrons. Now as then the tendrils of art and religion continue to twist and tangle, to rival, conspire, and vie.

Within each human life there are times one seeks religion for solace and other times one turns to art. The course of history also vacillates from one spiritual mode to the other. At the end of the nineteenth century Nietzsche declared God dead, and religion swooned while art took a radical turn into modernism, foreshowing the way of the future. Now, at the beginning of the third millennium, that earlier projected future has come and gone and religion is back, alive and screaming, while art languishes dormant as a bulb in winter, recouping energy for another burst.

VITA

The Facts

Throughout the history of sculpture, wood more often than not has taken a back seat to marble and bronze, the preferred media of the best of times. Wood, so easily available, seems more suited to popular and folk art with its too many imperfections, prone to parasites and bugs, vulnerable to rot and fire, and with an unnatural bent for witchery and the paranormal; all in all, a material fit for the worst of times.

Which, fortuitously, occurred following the sack of Rome, a period of tumult and cultural upheaval,

chaos and ruin, out of which the surviving stragglers
and motley conquerors began the Western world all
over again. Forests ripe for the cutting blanketed
the continent with abundant and accessible lumber
for new construction. Wood, with its roots buried
in pagan mysticism, bridged the gap between the
barbaric and the civilized, combining a savage
roughness with a potential for great finesse, a material
easily worked, durable and strong, responsive to
hacking, chopping, sawing and banging.

But even more portentous for the art of wood,
Christianity, aggressively on the rise, recognized
in wood the medium to personify resurrection. Aside
from its obvious relevance as material of the cross,
and more profoundly, the process of carving itself
involves the transformation of creation from destruction,
razing and raising, death and transfiguration. The
genius of the early Christian fathers lay in their
instinctive grasp of metaphor and mass psychology.
They saw the potential and seized their moment by
hiring the most talented artisans of the day to depict
their sacred message and voila! launched the most
successful advertising campaign of all time. Neither

the turbulence nor the magnificent carvings of the Middle Ages have since been equalled.

Following that stupendous burst of energy and raw exuberance the world settled down, harkened back to the classical world for inspiration, and during the following several centuries wood declined in artistic merit to that of supporting role, medium for decorative arts and crafts. But the inherent powers of wood take on many guises, and as man's great intellect strove to suppress womanly superstition, and science and technology ascended, gradually and almost imperceptibly, the imperfections of wood began to glow. This time it was the warmth and naturalness of wood that seemed somehow to cushion the dehumanizing effects of the advance of progress. The Arts and Crafts movement nurtured a nostalgia for simpler, pastoral, mythic times, and wooden artifacts took on an almost talismanic quality.

Now, we no longer take wood for granted but see forests as victims of clear cutting and decimation, of universal abuse. Environmentalists exhort us to stop the killing. Ecologists predict a dire future. New Age pundits counsel us to hug a tree. For sure, the next cultural cataclysm won't be spanned by a wooden bridge.

TEMPUS

FUGIT

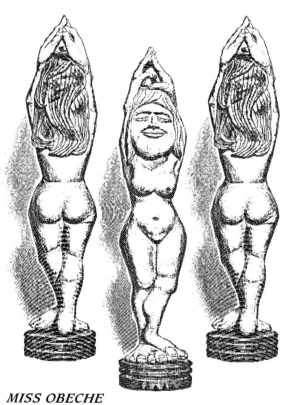

MISS OBECHE

The Choice

Deciding on a medium for art is much like finding a lover. Sometimes the die is cast early, as with childhood sweethearts who never waver. Other times one stumbles through a series of trials and errors and changing fancies. Sometimes one plots a course, other times love pops up unexpectedly. The foundation of art, as with life, rests on a bedrock of luck. For an enduring and productive union, so declares popular wisdom, there must be a compatible fit, the right tension and a healthy respect, and sometimes so it is, the art sprouts and blossoms over a long and fruitful career.

RUM TUM TUGGER

Other times the love sours, the affair ends, the marriage stagnates, the passion turns to boredom. There are many different kinds of attraction. Some arts demand a close collaboration between artist and medium. For others, rather than helpmeet, the mate the artist seeks is silent submission. What is more virginal and pure than a blank paper or canvas awaiting mastery? Little wonder writers and painters abound in such profusion. Of course, not all artists seek total domination, nor are all media so docile, available and affordable. For those who aspire to a more egalitarian partnership, musical instruments provide a mutuality based on ability and precision to attain the joyous realms. For those artists communally inclined there is theater, while singing appeals to the autogenous. Then there is dance exciting those drawn to a brutal physicality. Architecture stays the megalomanic. Film tempts the voyeuristic; conducting challenges the polygamous; collage delights the infantile; crafts absorb the steadfast and plodding. And sculpture? Sculpture mesmerizes the obstacle-oriented, those with a need to break down barriers, to butt heads on blocks of stone, defy crucibles of molten bronze, challenge nature's splinters and thorny pricks. To the wood sculptor, within that beach scrap so seemingly benign flickers a latent dazzle that lures the besotted carver as a flame beguiles the hapless moth.

MARY & MARY

ALLEGORY II

The Rub

I t is as easy to fall under wood's seductive spell as
to pick up a twig or trace the grain of a weathered
board. The carver, succumbing to wood's soporific
charm, serenely drifts into an earlier incarnation.
Even the basic tools, adz, chisel, gouge, mallet, rasp
and scraper, haven't changed from those wielded in
ancient times. The novice carver adopts the same
stance and working habits, practices the same
strokes and rhythms, develops the same skills and
stubborn patience. Drawing on common symbols

and motifs, she similarly perceives the universe by relating to a fuzzy past, far removed from present reality.

The carver's moment of truth comes with the adz gripped firmly and her arm raised high; she confronts the egregious question. Why? Why do it? Why hack up an object already beautiful of itself? Why desecrate a completed work of nature? The answer comes with a resounding thud, a violent act for which there is no justification and from which there is no retreat. The sensation emanating from that initial strike is a sickening one, and one the carver quickly buries under a flurry of succeeding blows, cuts, slices and chips. Do carvers come to grips with such brutality? Few admit sole culpability but try to implicate the wood as the one giving orders. It is the wood that "speaks," the flitch that desires transmutation, and the carver simply assists in collusion, or better, in collaboration. After all, as all carvers know, we think through our hands, not with our minds.

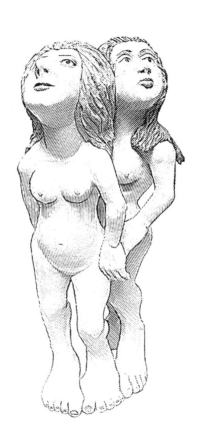

ERNESTINE,
DOLORES
&
PRUDENCE

The Lure

For my first carvings I used discarded wood,
refuse someone else had tossed out which, it
seemed to me, if I couldn't rehabilitate I also
couldn't further harm. All went well for a while,
but as my hands grew accustomed to the tools I
gradually began to hanker for new wood, real wood.
At night my dreams focussed on procurement of the
perfect flitch, immaculate, clean of debris, free from
knots, rusty nails and broken-off screws, uncorrupted

BLONDELL

by someone else's pathetic project, a piece with a
beautiful rich tone, a fine grain, one that would
hold a sharp edge, not too soft, not too hard. The
dream invaded my waking state and I lusted for
timber. At that time I lived in the east end of London
near a quay where exotic logs arrived. I browsed
among the gigantic trunks of lignum, rosewood, ebony
and coco bola, imbibed the flavors of the rain forests, and coveted the tiny pieces I bought as rare
gems, wrapping each one in red velvet. I developed
a scent for wood. In West Sussex I happened upon
the timber yard where Barbara Hepworth ordered
40-foot lime wood logs and I acquired a remnant from
one of her orders which later, after learning of the
tragic studio fire in which she perished, I was
tempted to sacrifice. But, it is not easy to give up a
piece of premium wood and instead, I hid it at the
bottom of my stack.

I visualized wood and wood arrived. An
acquaintance dropped off a 300-pound oak stump torn
up from widening the roadbed of the M23 motorway.
A friend sent a piece of olive from Jerusalem. Later,
in New York, I could sense wood inside dumpsters
even though buried by tons of debris, and I would
brashly descend into the iron tombs to retrieve the
treasures. Ending a trip to Brazil I threw out my

clothes and stuffed my luggage with flitches from
the Amazon. In Illinois I stoically ignored the
steamy hand caressing my ass because the dissolute
farmer owned a barn full of excellent walnut. I
tramped through woods and hauled out fallen
trunks; at night I removed beams from city demolition
sites; I dragged logs from drifted piles on remote
beaches; I searched, uncovered, recovered and
collected, forever on the lookout for that rare and
mythical piece that would yield its secrets in the
most sublime and transcendent statue of all.

The flitches became like family burdens,
overweight and needy, demanding and competitive,
each unique by touch and feel, each cherished and
despised, each wrapped and stacked in its place as I
awaited its moment to speak, to tell me it was
ready, ready to collude. And then, I would strike the
first blow and follow the strange course where a
knot in the wood throws off the hand that wields
the gouge that cuts yet another chip from the
wood's residuum, where a deviation of grain, a sud-
den sponginess, an insect's abandoned nest, a hole
or a split, distorts the image, exacts a change of

vision followed by a switch of strategy, freshly honed weapons, a renewed attack, and slowly the block mutates into an essence neither tree nor human, but an amalgamate of substance and spirits, past and present, death and life.

ALLEGORY I

GLORIA

The Twist

After moving to the West Coast in the mid-80s, the first piece I sold was Gloria. The purchaser proclaimed the little statue goddess of the house and set her prominently, although somewhat precariously, on the staircase baluster where she would command the entrance and all comings and goings. Perhaps it was a coincidence, perhaps a portent, but three months later the house burned down.

On October 7,1987, in San Diego, a disgruntled
worker set fire to the storage locker underneath unit
C-254 at Alacatraz Self-Storage, where a few days
before, during the interim while I was switching
studios, I had deposited my possessions and all
my work. The building was completely demolished,
the area restricted until assessed safe from further
combustion, and the blackened, oily rubble then
trucked to an undisclosed landfill.

FANNY

The Knell

There are many kinds of death, and each age contemplates the unknown according to current belief. Early on, monuments were raised to glorify the dead and, later, museums and libraries were erected to preserve the evidence of existence; it was believed that we transcend life by what we leave behind. Now, the repositories are filled to bursting and our present age grown cynical on so much stock-piled evidence. As children of latter day materialism we reckon the process of life in terms of diminishing returns: We depreciate in value until, unproductive and discounted, we're used up and worthless, good for nothing but to be buried under

a ton of dirt, or like noxious waste sealed up in a
concrete vault, or reduced to a handful of ash.
Raised on the virtue of extrinsic success the prospect
of our conclusive failure looms ever before us, moving
ever closer, ever larger. We mourn the passing of
time, our spent years, our wasted youth, our greying
hair, our missed opportunities, our bad luck, friends
lost track of, risks not taken, choices not made,
even to the grief we experience on finishing a good
book. To still our brooding natures we resolutely
build our individual histories, our personal repositories
of existence.

My history vanished with the fire, my inventory of
worth, and my life floated extraneous and superfluous.
But also, deep down inside, I detected an odd sense
of excitement. For sure, a phase of my life had
ended, but more than that, those tangled roots,
those obstacles and challenges, habits and routines
that for so long had bound me suddenly snapped
and, although I felt empty, I felt liberated. No longer
need I recoil from the thud of blows, the glint of
sharp blades, the staccato of successive taps, or the

ever mounting piles of chips, those curled slices of nature's skin that no amount of sweeping could remove. No longer need I restrain the impulse to throw down my tools and run.

APPLE MARY

*SELMA, MAVIS
& MOLLY*

The Essence

What is the definitive essence of wood if not resurrection? Through the purification of fire, perhaps Nature's ultimate revenge and pardon, the tree, flitch, carving and image disappear as their fibers transmute into ash, and along with them any attendant spirits innocuously evaporate. The wind blows the ash and in time it settles and seeps into the earth where it adds nutrients, and where, with a measure of water, it yields clay, the basic element of life. And life begins again.

Clay

Pandora was made of clay, and, even though her klutz of a husband smashed up her store of worldly knowledge, she still held on to Hope. And the feel of clay truly does impart a life-affirming sense of hope, well-being and healing. Moist clay will draw out poisons, soothe stings and burns, revitalize the skin, calm the nerves and restore energy. Yet, no one is about to walk around squeezing a handful of mud. There is no totemic value to clay, and crumbling a beach clod in the hand will never precipitate the seductive spell cast by a driftwood scrap. There is no artifice to clay, no baggage, no tangled roots, no dark secrets, no demands, no resistance; but, matrix of mud pies and retreat of wallowing pigs, clay is safe and welcoming as the monolithic mushy womb of Mother Nature herself.

Virtually indestructible, clay's plasticity conforms to all pressures. Model it up, knock it down, begin again, no matter. When it sags a short rest will restore it, when it dries out a good soak will bring it back and, fire-friendly, even vitrified shards can be ground into grog for another batch. There is no waste, no desecration, clay is neither a precious nor endangered element, but abundant everywhere and supremely regenerative.

For some sculptors, clay is too maternal, lacks machismo, not resistant enough for real sculpture, not fierce enough for making fetish figures. Rather, its utility lies in expediency, a cheap means for sketching, working out ideas, making studies and maquettes. Then there is clay's practical side: adobe bricks and mud huts, crafts and vessels, all the vulgar characteristics guaranteed to befoul any fine art reputation. In the hierarchy of high art, clay sinks to the bottom.

Of course, fashions of belief change with the evolutionary seasons. Not all societies are so mercilessly materialistic as ours. In earlier times clay tomb figures functioned as holders for the spirit as well as provided company for and served the needs of the deceased on their journey to the next world. Those simple surrogate statuettes acted when and where the living could not; they symbolized the eternal, provided a link, mitigated the anguish, neutralized the specter, and filled the void.

In our present era it takes a special temperament to model clay; probably the very young and the very old understand best its special qualities, those whose egos have yet to bloom or already have blown with the wind; those with nothing to prove, nothing at stake or, beyond failure, are free to let go.

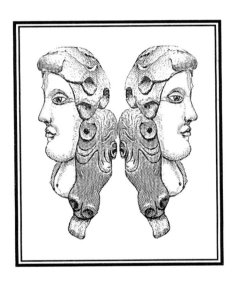

Epilogue

Whenever I look at the other side of the road, it appears greener than the side I'm standing on, and many times I have crossed back and forth to check out the veracity of this phenomenon. And yes, it is true: the other side really is greener. Chickens are wise and have always known this. For it is only with distance that we see clearly, take in the whole picture, are able to perceive the rainbow. So, after the fire and a time of brooding on the ashes at my feet, my eyes began to seek a clarity, and the gnaw to escape from Southern California grew unbearable. I wanted to bolt from the dry desert and fiery sun to the other unspoilt, memory-free . . . greener side.

Perhaps it was time for me to make my peace with trees, to put down my hatchet and sort out my ambivalence, to take another look. And on the Olympic Peninsula, the most northwesterly point of the country, there was much to take in. The forests here are green, very green. And they are real, not the domesticated regimented rows of orchards and groves of the south, not imported ornamentals that mysteriously pop up overnight in malls and housing tracts, but here the forests are ancient, vast, dark and silent, the trees regal and tall, the canopy dense and the ground beneath cushiony, chaste of scruffy underbrush; lovely for walking and for musing; comforting and enticing, so easy to wander, so easy to forget the civilized world, so easy to lose oneself completely.

It doesn't take long to realize that trees are female, primevally maternal, nurturers of flora and fauna, wild life and fungi. Of all living matter trees alone provide our human essentials: shelter, food, water, clothing, fire, even paper for doodling; our great bounteous and prolific Mother anticipated all our needs.

In this temperate rain forest there is the curiosity of nurse trees; trees that have fallen and from which, over time, saplings issue, their roots circled around the nurse trunk like hugging babies holding on. And not just one tree will sprout, but an entire row will grow down the length of a trunk like a suckling litter of kittens. The moss that hangs from the branches is dry, like over-permed hair. It is not possible to look at these trees without seeing women.

And what is more female than a tree's crotch where two branches or trunks divide like thighs and in between a lovely Mound of Venus reigns. Some are so incredibly realistic, so anatomically correct, so sexy. Perhaps one of nature's jokes? In the local museum there is a photo of a wild-eyed woodsman standing in front of his cabin behind a fence of such provocative crotches. And, what better magic to stagger the uninvited guest than a hedge of burly maternal pudenda?

And what better illustrates, and on a cosmic scale, the battered woman than man's long history of beating up the woods? It is the National Parks that, like medieval nunneries, now offer protection to their inhabitants, shelters for the silent orders clustered behind the high walls of federal law and regulation. Yet, outside, greedy eyes watch and plot and wait to plunder, rape, subjugate, control, and devastate . . . such is the history of woods and of women.

Yet, trees are no Madonnas. In storm weather when the winds pick up, watching a stand of trees begin to gyrate induces a nervousness, and as the winds build, a rising fear, and in a full-blown storm, a catapult into the eye of a Dionysian tempest. Of course, after so much nurturing, the great Mothers deserve to let off some steam, and caught up in the raging wind they do; swaying and twisting, writhing wildly, leaves and needles flying, limbs cracking, out of control, madly dancing in a frenzy as though they're about to tear their children to bits. The crack of a snapped trunk and the smash of crashing branches instills an abject terror.

* * *

On the Peninsula, there are several different forests. In the National Park, the well-maintained trails and facilities provide a prudent taste of nature for everyone: from picnickers who struggle with hampers and coolers and after gorging themselves lie back contentedly under the shade of an ancient tree, to serious hikers with backpacks full of survival gear who, leaving nothing to chance, set off at a brisk pace for many, many miles to reach a mark on their charts, a respectable goal. For these hikers, trees have no more importance than indicating the edges of trails, that meaningless space beyond the black lines on the maps they so resolutely follow. For tourists with no picnics on which to feast and no desire to huff and puff up monotonous trails, there are gift shop postcard racks to twirl and a pinecone souvenir to buy.

Another forest lies deep in the interior of the Park, far removed from the trails and facilities, and contains the best examples of what remains of old growth in a pristine environment. And spreading beyond Park boundaries there are the forests of leased government land or those held in private hands;

forests abused, forgotten, or temporarily overlooked. What trails exist in these woods are hard to find, overgrown logging roads or animal paths that lead to nowhere in particular. A walk through these forests can be a most fazing experience. There are no guide posts, maps, sign-in books, or watchful rangers; no one to keep track of who's going where. An uncharted forest is forbidden territory to all but the most seasoned of explorers, or to the extremely foolish.

And should we foolishly venture in, we will find ourselves in a very strange place indeed, and it won't take long to realize that we are the aliens in a baffling world. Our eyes will search in vain for trustworthy landmarks where all the trees look alike. And where around us the quiet grows to a roar. Even the sounds of our own footfalls can't break through the silence, yet the vibration of our feet striking the forest floor rebounds upward through our bodies. We feel our center of gravity shift. There is no horizon to stabilize us, only tantalizing sparkles bouncing lightly through the canopy. Trusting to luck, we foolishly forfeit our sense of direction, lose sight of our purpose, and gradually begin to walk in circles. We sink into an altered state meandering in Nature's vast womb, at one with the trees and the eons. We feel drugged. We stumble on in circles within circles, doing our forty days in the wilderness, tripping down to Hades without looking back, until . . . until . . .

Plunging directly into the woods, like jumping into the middle of a lake, is the shock way of confronting the unknown, one jump ahead of paralysis, and sometimes that leap-now-think-later advance works. Sometimes. Sometimes a half-crazed hiker blunders out, and those who don't make it, no one knows about.

* * *

Fortunately, there is a gentler way, the *poco a poco* approach: first the toe, then the ankle, then a retreat, and begin again. In this way, very slowly and gradually, we meet the trees, an undifferentiated mass at first, and later, individually as we grow familiar with a small area before moving deeper in, never losing sight of the way out. For that is what happens; the trees separate from the forest, certain ones stand out, the bolder ones initially and then the shyer ones, for some trees definitely are more imposing than others, some more independent while others lean or snuggle up to the stronger. The old ones stoop, the young shoot up and each suggests a personality. Anthropomorphism is endemic to forest haunts. Our vision clears. Snags riddled with holes rise as apartment houses for birds and rodents. Patterns emerge; a recognizable environ takes shape. And not just visually but subtly sounds arise from the silence; rustlings, the play of the breeze among the branches, tiny crackings as old twigs break, creakings like ships heaving in heavy seas as the old forest matrons adjust their stiffened positions, the plopping of raindrops that seep through the canopy,

the odd chirp. Single trees stand out as sentinels
and the accompanying sounds take on a meaning
as well, and together, the sights, sounds, and
aromatics of fir, cedar and spruce form a language
for which we reach way back into our deepest
recesses to try to understand. For the forest, like
Cassandra, is telling us things we should know yet
are afraid to hear.

If at one time the goddesses did rule supreme,
then perhaps the ethereality we sense in the forest
comes from them. For sure the great trunks that
rise like pillars remind us of temples, but temples
and pillars bespeak the mighty symbols of man's
immutable beliefs, and these woods harken to an
earlier time of transformation and metamorphosis;
a time before covenants and laws, avenging gods,
retribution, holy wars, oppression, a place timeless,
a purity that, obviously, couldn't last. Perhaps our
sense of immanence reaches to that original crotch
from which art and religion tried to split as though
one were independent of the other. In the forest
they remain fused, deep spirituality and consummate
beauty.

In the midst of a forest glade there are no roads to excite our wanderlust, beckoning us to follow to wherever they might lead, to ponder the greener of their sides. Here, when we sit quietly, attentively, we find the scales of everyday abstraction waft away as so much superfluous fluff, irrelevant and unnecessary. It is in these small, dwindling preserves, enchanted enclaves, we find a resting place out of time that awakens our souls, and we breathe in the harmony of our ancient inner peace.

ELFREDA

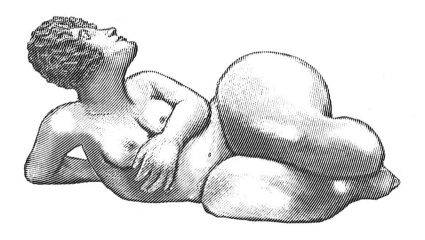

Plates

Allegory I, 1973
Limewood, 25.5 x 9.5 x 4"
10/7/87

Allegory II, 1973-4
Limewood, 30 x 22"
10/7/87

Apple Mary, 1972
Apple, 10.25"
Collection of Margaret Davidson

Baby J, 1974
Oak, 34 x 17"
10/7/87

Blondell, 1976
Pine, 12"
Collection of Jane Plum

Fanny, 1984-6
Bronze, 5 x 6"
10/7/87

Elfreda, 1983
Walnut, 16 x 32"
10/7/87

Ernestine, Dolores & Prudence, 1983
Pine, 30"
10/7/87

Eve, 1978
Walnut, 43.5"
10/7/87

Gloria, 1975
Beech, 15.5"
Collection of Ingrid Croce

Helen, Violet & Edna, 1973
Limewood, 23.5 x 15"
10/7/87

Lady on a Turtle, 1983
Walnut, 12.25 x 11.5"
10/7/87

Mary & Mary, 1972
Brazilian rosewood, 14.5"
10/7/87

Miss Num, 1973
Lignum vitae, 18"
Collection of Janet L. Brown

Miss Obeche, 1972
Obeche, 18.5"
Collection of John B. Hamilton

Rum Tum Tugger, 1977
Rosa peroba, 21.25"
Collection of the artist

St. Mark, 1972
Brazilian rosewood, 8.5"
Collection of Ingrid Bohle

Selma, Mavis & Molly, 1974
Basswood, 17"
10/7/87

Tempus Fugit, 1984
Basswood, 20.5 x 12.5"
10/7/87

Vita, 1972
Lignam vitae, 15"
Collection of Edward Field & Neil Derrick

Wise & Foolish Virgins, 1974
Butternut, 23 x 11.5"
Returned to artist by Leslie L. Brown

VITA

WISE & FOOLISH VIRGINS–view 1

WISE & FOOLISH VIRGINS–view 2

SELMA, MAVIS & MOLLY

MISS NUM

GLORIA

MARY & MARY

ALLEGORY I–view 1

ALLEGORY I–detail 1

ALLEGORY I–detail 2

ELFREDA

ERNESTINE, DOLORES & PRUDENCE–view 1

ERNESTINE, DOLORES & PRUDENCE–view 2

ALLEGORY II–view 1

ALLEGORY II–view 2

EVE

EVE–detail

HELEN, VIOLET & EDNA–view 1

HELEN, VIOLET & EDNA–view 2

TEMPUS

FUGIT

BABY J

BABY J–detail

LADY ON A TURTLE

About the Artist

Diane Derrick was born in central California in 1934 and was raised on a ranch. After art school and college, she immediately went to New York where she lived on and off for twenty-five years, working at various clerical jobs and intermittently traveling to and living in Europe and New England, writing short stories and plays. In the late 60s she began sculpting and subsequently had shows in London, Dusseldorf, Chicago, Portland, Oregon, and San Diego, California. In the 80s, she and her partner, Olivia Alfano, built a small three-story house and studio inside a barn in rural Illinois. Presently they reside on the Olympic Peninsula in Washington State.